TEA *for* TWO

Taking Time *for* Friends

A Special Gift

FOR:

Clayne

FROM:

Bernadette

DATE:

12 · 12 · 95

Happy Birthday

TEA
for
TWO

Edited by:
Paul C. Brownlow

Brownlow

Brownlow Publishing Company, Inc.

Tea for Two

Originally the phrase, "tea for two," was an English street cry in the eighteenth century that vendors used to advertise their bargain-priced tea. Normally a pot of tea was *thruppence*, but enterprising souls hungry for more business would often lower it to *tuppence* by shouting, "Tea for two!"

Today the phrase has come to mean so much more. It now speaks of a cozy time for friends to relax, to enjoy the moment, unburden themselves for an hour or two, and share their lives together.

TEA IS "SECOND" ONLY TO WATER

*A*ccording to *Erh Ya*, an ancient Chinese dictionary dating back to 350 B.C., tea was first cultivated in Szechwan, then along the Yangtze River, down to the sea. It was cultivated commercially by the first century A.D. In the 1600s the Dutch opened tea plantations in Java and imported tea to Europe. Legend has it that the first tea to reach England arrived with a British admiral who had captured a Dutch ship and discovered the tea in its galley. Now tea is second only to water as the world's most popular drink, as well as the least expensive.

CREAM SCONES

INGREDIENTS

2 cups flour sifted with

3 teaspoons baking powder

½ teaspoon salt

2 tablespoons sugar

¼ cup butter

½ cup cream

2 beaten eggs

COOKING INSTRUCTIONS

- Cut butter into sifted dry ingredients. Combine eggs and cream and add.

- Pat to ¾-inch thick.

- Cut in squares or triangles, sprinkle with sugar and bake at 375° until lightly brown, about 20 minutes.

- Serve hot with any jams, preserves or Traditional Tea Spreads (see page 29).

Yield: 1 dozen

The most agreeable of all companions is a simple, frank person, without any high pretensions to an oppressive greatness—one who loves life, and understands the use of it; obliging alike at all hours; above all, of a golden temper, and steadfast as an anchor. For such an one we gladly exchange the greatest genius, the most brilliant wit, the profoundest thinker.

GOTTHOLD EPHRAIM LESSING

Partnership is not a principle, but a relationship between persons who share in a common enterprise, involving common risks, common privileges, and common responsibilities. Everything depends on the reality of our partnership with one another and of each of us with God.

GEORGE CRAIG STEWART

Being with people you like and respect is so meaningful. Perhaps you have known some of them most of your life. Having friends around for a pleasant evening is one of life's most cherished joys as far as I am concerned. But when those with me are fellow believers how much greater that joy is, for we know that it will be rekindled, one day, in eternity.

JAMES STEWART

Tea at Green Gables

"I don't really know if I'm doing right—it may make you more addlepated than ever—but you can ask Diana to come over and spend the afternoon with you and have tea here."

"Oh, Marilla!" Anne clasped her hands. "How perfectly lovely! You *are* able to imagine things after all or else you'd never have understood how I've longed for that very thing. It will seem so nice and grown-uppish. No fear of my forgetting to put the tea to draw when I have company. Oh, Marilla, can I use the rosebud spray tea set?"

"No, indeed! The rosebud tea set! Well, what next? You know I never use that except for the minister or the ladies' club. You'll put down the old brown tea set. But you can open the little yellow crock of cherry preserves. It's time it was being used anyhow—I believe it's beginning to work. And you can cut some fruitcake and have some of the cookies and snaps."

"I can just imagine myself sitting down at the head of the table and pouring out the tea," said Anne, shutting her eyes ecstatically. "And asking Diana if she takes sugar! I know she doesn't but of course I'll ask her just as if I didn't know. And then pressing her to take another piece of fruitcake and another helping of preserves. Oh, Marilla, it's a wonderful sensation just to think of it. Can I take her into the spare room to lay off her hat when she comes? And then into the parlor to sit?"

"No. The sitting-room will do for you and your company. But there's a bottle half full of raspberry cordial that was left over from the church social the other night. It's on the second shelf of the sitting-room closet and you and Diana can have it if you like, and a cooky to eat with it along in the afternoon, for I daresay Matthew'll be late coming in to tea since he's hauling potatoes to the vessel."

Anne flew down to the hollow, past the Dryad's Bubble and up the spruce path to Orchard Slope, to ask Diana to tea. As a result, just after Marilla had driven off to Carmody, Diana came over, dressed in her second best dress and looking exactly as it is proper to look when asked out to tea. At other times she was wont to run into the kitchen without knocking; but now she knocked primly at the front door. And when Anne, dressed in her second best, as primly opened it, both little girls shook hands as gravely as if they had never met before. This unnatural solemnity lasted until after Diana had been taken to the east gable to lay off her hat and then had sat for ten minutes in the sitting room, toes in position.

"How is your mother?" inquired Anne politely, just as if she had not seen Mrs. Barry picking apples that morning in excellent health and spirits.

"She is very well, thank you. I suppose Mr. Cuthbert is hauling potatoes to the *Lily Sands* this afternoon, is he?" said Diana, who had ridden down to Mr. Harmon Andrews' that morning in Matthew's cart.

"Yes. Our potato crop is very good this year. I hope your father's potato crop is good, too."

"It is fairly good, thank you. Have you picked many of your apples yet?"

"Oh, ever so many," said Anne, forgetting to be dignified and jumping up quickly. "Let's go out to the orchard and get some of the Red Sweetings, Diana. Marilla says we can have all that are left on the tree. Marilla is a very generous woman. She said we could have fruitcake and cherry preserves for tea. But it isn't good manners to tell your company what you are going to give them to eat, so I won't tell you what she said we could have to drink. Only it begins with an r and a c and it's a bright red color. I love bright red drinks, don't you? They taste twice as good as any other color."

LUCY MAUD MONTGOMERY

The Love of a Friend

Because you love me, I have found
New joys that were not mine before;
New stars have lightened up my sky
With glories growing more and more.

Because you love me I can rise
To the heights of fame and realms of power;
Because you love me I may learn
The highest use of every hour.

Because you love me I can choose
To look through your dear eyes and see
Beyond the beauty of the Now
Far onward to Eternity.

Because you love me I can wait
With perfect patience well possessed;
Because you love me all my life
Is circled with unquestioned rest;
Yes, even Life and even Death
Is all unquestioned and all blest.

ANONYMOUS

Life is made up, not of great sacrifices or duties, but of little things in which smiles and kindness and small obligations, given habitually, are what win and preserve the heart and secure comfort.

SIR HUMPHRY DAVY

In the eighteenth century, tea became an institution, partly with a boost from Queen Anne, who reigned from 1702 to 1714. She started the custom of drinking tea instead of ale for breakfast. She is also credited with originating the use of a large silver teapot instead of the small Chinese ceramic ones.

Blessed is the servant who loves his brother as much when he is sick and useless as when he is well and can be of service to him. And blessed is he who loves his brother as well when he is afar off as when he is by his side, and who would say nothing behind his back he might not, in love, say before his face.

FRANCIS OF ASSISI

Surely there is no more beautiful sight to see in all this world,—full as it is of beautiful adjustments and mutual ministrations,—than the growth of two friends' natures who, as they grow old together, are always fathoming, with newer needs, deeper depths of each other's life, and opening richer veins of one another's helpfulness.

PHILLIPS BROOKS

Because of a friend, life is a little stronger, fuller, more gracious thing for the friend's existence, whether she be near or far. If the friend is close at hand, that is best; but if she is far away she still is there to think of, to wonder about, to hear from, to write to, to share life and experience with, to serve, to honor, to admire, to love.

ARTHUR CHRISTOPHER BENSON

The glory of friendship is not the outstretched hand, nor the kindly smile, nor the joy of companionship; it is the spiritual inspiration that comes to one when he discovers that someone believes in him and is willing to trust him with his friendship.

RALPH WALDO EMERSON

Understanding

If I knew you and you knew me,

If both of us could clearly see,

And with an inner sight divine

The meaning of your heart and mine,

I'm sure that we would differ less,

And clasp our hands in friendliness;

Our thoughts would pleasantly agree

If I knew you and you knew me.

NIXON WATERMAN

The Queen of Tea

Queen Victoria did love her tea. During her reign, the East India Company of London controlled the world's supply of tea and thus the Queen always had the choicest blends and the freshest supplies from the first clipper ship into port annually.

At the palace, tea was served from the Queen's favorite silver tea service. It is still in use today, even though most British tea lovers agree that a china teapot makes a better cup of tea than anybody's silver—even the Queen's. Footmen would roll in the tea trolleys and the butler would pour tea for the accumulated guests.

However, for a family tea the Queen herself would begin pouring with the question, "Shall I be Mum?" instead of, "Shall I pour?" We are told that this endearing custom continues to this day.

Endeavor to be always patient of the faults and imperfections of others, for thou hast many faults and imperfections of thy own that require a reciprocation of forbearance. If thou art not able to make thyself that which thou wishest to be, how canst thou expect to mould another in conformity to thy will?

THOMAS À KEMPIS

Once I found a dear friend. "Dear me," I said, "he was made for me." But now I find more and more friends who seem to have been made for me, and more and yet more made for me. Is it possible we were all made for each other all around the world?

G. K. CHESTERTON

The Friend Who Just Stands By

When trouble comes your soul to try,
You love the friend who just "stands by."
Perhaps there's nothing he can do—
The thing is strictly up to you;
For there are troubles all your own,
And paths the soul must tread alone;
Times when love cannot smooth the road
Nor friendship lift the heavy load,
But just to know you have a friend
Who will "stand by" until the end,
Whose sympathy through all endures,
Whose warm handclasp is always yours—
It helps, some ways, to pull you through,
Although there's nothing he can do.
And so with fervent heart you cry,
"God bless the friend who just 'stands by.'"

B. Y. WILLIAMS

CRUMPETS

INGREDIENTS

2 teaspoons yeast

1 teaspoon sugar

¼ cup warm water

⅓ cup milk

1 egg, lightly beaten

4 tablespoons butter, melted, divided

1 cup all-purpose flour

½ teaspoon salt

COOKING INSTRUCTIONS

- Mix yeast with sugar; add water and let stand about 5 minutes, until foamy. Stir in milk, egg and 1 tablespoon butter.

- Add flour and salt; mix until well blended. Cover with damp towel and let stand in warm place about 45 minutes, or until almost doubled in volume.

- Brush four 3-inch flan rings and bottom of heavy frying pan with remaining melted butter. Heat over low flame and place 2 tablespoons of batter inside each ring.

- Cook for 7 minutes, or until tops are dry and holes appear. Remove rings and turn crumpets. Cook about 2 minutes, or until bottoms are lightly browned. Repeat with remaining batter.

- Serve warm with preserves and Devonshire cream.

Yield: 7 dozen

TRADITONAL TEA SPREADS

Devonshire Cream

Orange Marmalade

Strawberry Jam

Honey

Cinnamon and Sugar

Apple Butter

Strawberry Butter

Raspberry Preserves

Apricot Preserves

Apple Chutney

The cozy fire is bright and gay,

The merry kettle boils away

And hums a cheerful song.

I sing the saucer and the cup;

Pray, Mary, fill the teapot up,

And do not make it strong.

BARRY PAIN

I Shall Not
Pass Again This Way

The bread that bringeth strength I want to give,
The water pure that bids the thirsty live:
I want to help the fainting day by day;
I'm sure I shall not pass again this way.

I want to give the oil of joy for tears,
The faith to conquer crowding doubts and fears.
Beauty for ashes may I give alway:
I'm sure I shall not pass again this way.

I want to give good measure running o'er,
And into angry hearts I want to pour
The answer soft that turneth wrath away;
I'm sure I shall not pass again this way.

I want to give to others hope and faith,
I want to do all that the Master saith;
I want to live aright from day to day;
I'm sure I shall not pass again this way.

AUTHOR UNKNOWN

GINGERSNAPS

INGREDIENTS

1 cup molasses

½ cup butter

1 teaspoon soda

1 tablespoon boiling water

1½ cups flour

½ teaspoon salt

1½ teaspoons ginger

½ teaspoon cinnamon

Sugar for sprinkling

COOKING INSTRUCTIONS

- Bring molasses and butter to boil in sauce pan. Cool. Add soda mixed with boiling water to molasses mixture and stir.

- Sift 2 cups of flour with salt and spices into mixing bowl. Stir in molasses mixture. Add remaining flour to make dough. Chill. Roll dough very thin on a lightly floured board. Sprinkle with sugar and cut with 2-inch round cookie cutter. Bake on ungreased cookie sheets at 375° about 5 minutes or until set.

Yield: 7 dozen

TEA CONQUERS COFFEE IN ENGLAND

*D*id you know that the English were coffee drinkers when the East India Company began importing tea to England? Tea conquered the coffee habit in a few short years. But, dear as it became to the English, for the first hundred years tea was a novel treat only for the very rich. It wasn't until the close of the seventeenth century, when imports were up to 20,000 pounds a year, that enough tea was available for almost everyone to have a cup a day.

When the English taste for tea outdid coffee and made a dent in the ale trade, Parliament levied tax on tea. Despite the expense, tea was something the British could no longer live without.

My Hand Clasped in Thine

The joy of meeting makes us love farewell;
We gather once again around the hearth,
And thou will tell
All that thy keen experience has been
Of pleasure, danger, misadventure, mirth,
And unforeseen.

But friend, go not again so far away;
In need of some small help I always stand,
Come whatso may;
I know not whither leads this path of mine,
But I can tread it better when my hand
Is clasped in thine.

ALFRED DE MUSSET

A Child's Kiss

A child's kiss
Set on thy sighing lips
shall make thee glad;
A poor man served by thee
shall make thee rich;
A sick man helped by thee
shall make thee strong;
Thou shalt be served thyself
by every sense
Of service which thou renderest.

ELIZABETH BARRETT BROWNING

Walk With Me

If you have learned to walk
A little more sure-footedly than I,
Be patient with my stumbling then
And know that only as I do my best and try
May I attain the goal
For which we both are striving.

If through experience, your soul
Has gained heights which I
As yet in dim-lit vision see,
Hold out your hand and point the way,
Lest from its straightness I should stray,
And walk a mile with me.

ANONYMOUS

Like China

The finest china in the world is burned at least three times, some of it more than three times. Dresden china is always burned three times. Why does it go through that intense fire?

Once ought to be enough; twice ought to be enough. No, three times are necessary to burn that china so that the gold and the crimson are brought out more beautiful and then fastened there to stay. We are fashioned after the same principle in human life. Our trials are burned into us once, twice, thrice; and by God's grace these beautiful colors are there and they are there to stay forever.

CORTLAND MYERS

Of Teacups and Friends

Have you ever really looked at teacups and saucers? There are many similarities among them, yet many differences. Some cups and saucers are perfectly matched, while others are not. The "mismatched" ones have been brought together by a curious happenstance of time and need.

A number are dainty and delicate and appear to be too fragile to use. Others are sturdy and appear to be strong—what my grandmother would have referred to as "wholesome."

Some give the appearance of being flawless—no chips, cracks, or imperfections. Others have obvious flaws that are visible to anyone who glances in their direction. There are even those that have been shattered, only to have been lovingly, even painstakingly, repaired and mended, now ready to serve again.

Many cups are beautiful to behold in style and decor with colors from the rainbow. Can you imagine how boring it would be if

they were all the same color? Others are plain in appearance — or worse, they seem to have no beauty at all to the casual observer.

Perhaps you have a cup-and-saucer set that is very expensive, even rare. Or, maybe you have in your possession a very inexpensive, common set — one that looks just like all the others and sort of "blends in" with the group.

Some are brand new — never even used for the purpose for which they were intended, but anxious to serve. Some have been used countless times, with many opportunities to serve still in their future.

Many cups are easy to hold. They fit in your hand perfectly! So easy to use, so accommodating. A few are awkward; they don't feel comfortable; they are just downright difficult to handle.

Some claim they have "served their time." They are chipped, worn, and would just like to sit on the shelf and be admired for their work. But others want to be used until the very end, fearful that they will be put on the shelf and forgotten. And have you noticed? Some are capable of holding much more than others.

Some are part of a set with many matching pieces. A number

are one of a kind—unique—not part of a set, but wanting to belong to the group.

Some can be tossed into the dishwasher—"DURABLE," they say. Others must be treated gently—"HAND-WASHED," not subjected to severe changes in temperature.

Some cups are everyone's favorites—always chosen and ever popular. Some are almost never selected. In fact, they are often overlooked.

Yet, with all of their many differences and similarities, all cups and saucers were designed for a common purpose. Perhaps you have heard and in all probability have even used the phrase, "tea service." You see, cups and saucers were created to serve.

Teacups and friends?—the comparison is obvious. We too have many similarities, many differences, many unique characteristics. We are all different, yet all needed. Fortunately, it takes all of us, each with her own gifts and talents, to serve the needs of God's children.

Next time you pick up a teacup, think of a friend.

LINDA GAITHER

There are
veins in the hills
where jewels hide
And gold lies buried deep;
There are harbor-towns
where the great ships ride,
And fame and fortune sleep;
But land and sea
though we tireless rove,
And follow each trail to the end,
Whatever the wealth of our treasure-trove,
The best we shall find is a friend.

JOHN J. MOMENT

Who Is Your Friend?

- She who understands your silence.

- She who will be a balance in the seesaw of life.

- She who considers your needs before your deservings.

- She who to herself is true and therefore must be so to you.

- She who, when she reaches the top of the ladder, does not forget you if you are at the bottom.

- She who is the same today when prosperity smiles upon you and tomorrow when adversity and sorrows come.

- She who cheerfully comes in when all the world has gone out, who weeps with you when the laughing is away.

- She who guards your interests as her own, neither flatters nor deceives, gives just praise to your good deeds, and equally condemns your bad acts.

- She who is the same to you in the society of the wealthy and proud as in the solitude of poverty, whose cheerful smile sheds sunshine in every company.

She is your friend.

Think of Me as Your Friend

Think of me as your friend, I pray,
And call me by a loving name;
I will not care what others say,
If only you remain the same.
I will not care how dark the night,
I will not care how wild the storm,
Your love will fill my heart with light
And shield me close and keep me warm.

Think of me as your friend, I pray,
For else my life is little worth:
So shall your memory light my way,
Although we meet no more on earth.
For while I know your faith secure,
I ask no happier fate to see:
Thus to be loved by one so pure
Is honor rich enough for me.

WILLIAM WINTER

We all belong to each other, but friendship is the especial accord of one life with a kindred life. We tremble at the threshold of any new friendship with awe and wonder and fear lest it should not be real or, believing that it is, lest we should prove ourselves unworthy of the solemn and holy contact of life with life, of soul with soul. We cannot live unworthy lives in the constant presence of noble beings to whom we belong and who believe that we are at least endeavoring after nobleness.

RALPH WALDO EMERSON

Have you ever had your day suddenly turn sunshiny because of a cheerful word? Have you ever wondered if this could be the same world, because someone had been unexpectedly kind to you? You can make today the same for somebody. It is only a question of a little imagination, a little time and trouble. Think now, "What can I do today to make someone happy?"—old persons, children, servants—even a bone for the dog, or sugar for the bird! Why not?

MALTBIE D. BABCOCK

Two are better than one. If one falls down, his friend can help him up. But pity the man who falls and has no one to help him up!

ECCLESIASTES 4:9-10

People who have warm friends are healthier and happier than those who have none. A single real friend is a treasure worth more than gold or precious stones. Money can buy many things, good and evil. All the wealth of the world could not buy you a friend or pay you for the loss of one.

G. D. PRENTICE

There can be no real and abiding happiness without sacrifice. Our greatest joys do not result from our efforts toward self-gratification, but from a loving and spontaneous service to other lives. Joy comes not to him who seeks it for himself, but to him who seeks it for other people.

H. W. SYLVESTER

So What Is Tea, Really?

*I*ndigenous to China, Tibet and Northern India, the tea plant (*Camellia sinensis*) is a shrubby evergreen. Left alone, it grows to 30 feet and bears fragrant white flowers. Tea planters prune it to three to five feet for convenience in harvesting. The best teas are grown in mountains to 6,000 feet. Perfect conditions for the flavor and quality include an average shade temperature of 65° and well-distributed rainfall of 100 inches a year, with long intervals of sun in-between showers. Now, three-fourths of the world's tea comes from India and Sri Lanka. It also grows in Java and Formosa, as well as in China and Tibet. The beverage is made from dried tea leaves.

LEMON CURD

*A delicious, easy-to-make sweet
lemon butter that is used as a
spread on crumpets, muffins, and toast.*

INGREDIENTS

3 large lemons

5 eggs

1 cup granulated sugar

8 tablespoons unsalted butter

COOKING INSTRUCTIONS

Grate the lemon rinds and set aside. Squeeze the juice and put into
a blender or food processor. Add the remaining ingredients and
process until smooth. Pour the mixture into a very heavy sauce pan
or the top half of a double boiler. Stir in the lemon rind and cook
over low heat or over simmering water for about 10 minutes, until
thickened. Stir the mixture with a wire whisk if it appears lumpy.
Chill the lemon curd before serving; it becomes thicker as it cools.

Yield: 1⅓ cups

What a wretched lot of old shrivelled creatures we shall be by-and-by. Never mind—the uglier we get in the eyes of others, the lovelier we shall be to each other; that has always been my firm faith about friendship, and now it is in a slight degree my experience.

GEORGE ELIOT

There are few hours in life more agreeable than the hour dedicated to the ceremony known as afternoon tea.

HENRY JAMES

Do not forsake your friend and the friend of your father.

PROVERBS 27:10

Tea and Temperance

The social progress of tea in Britain was given a large boost by the Temperance Movement, which planned large "tea meetings" and promoted it as a nonalcoholic alternative to the more popular gin and ale. But not all temperance supporters were tea lovers. John Wesley preached against tea as a waste of money that could be spent by the poor for food. And the well-to-do families could use their tea money to support teachers or other charitable causes. However, during a prolonged illness, Wesley turned to tea and became quite fond of it. He was even given a large china teapot by Thomas Wedgewood, the porcelain maker.

The Perfect Cup of Tea

Perfect tea requires only a few simple elements:

- "Hot the pot." Pour hot water into a ceramic teapot and let it sit until time to use.

- Using cool, fresh tap water, fill the kettle and bring it to a boil.

- As the water in the kettle is about to boil, empty the teapot, dry it and measure into it 1 teaspoonful of tea per cup plus "one for the pot." Tea bags may be substituted if you prefer.

- Just as the water has come to a full, rolling boil, bring the "pot to the kettle" and place it next to the stove. If the water continues to boil, it will become flat and decrease the flavor of the tea. So, immediately pour water over the tea leaves.

- Put a lid on the teapot, cover it with a tea cozy and let steep for 5 minutes. Stir once during the steeping process. Using a strainer, pour tea into cups and serve.

A Quiet Friendship

The very best thing is good talk, and the thing that helps it most is friendship. How it dissolves the barriers that divide us, and loosens all constraints, and diffuses itself through all the veins of life—this feeling that we understand and trust each other, and wish each other heartily well!

Everything into which it really comes is good. It transforms letter writing from a task to a pleasure. It makes music a thousand times more sweet. The people who play and sing not at us, but to us, how delightful it is to listen to them! Yes, there is a talkability that can express itself even without words. There is an exchange of thoughts and feeling which is happily alike in speech and in silence. It is quietness pervaded with friendship.

HENRY VAN DYKE

We can survive functional illiteracy or shattered windows of vulnerability, but not the demise of "the decent cup of tea."

MALACHI MCCORMICK

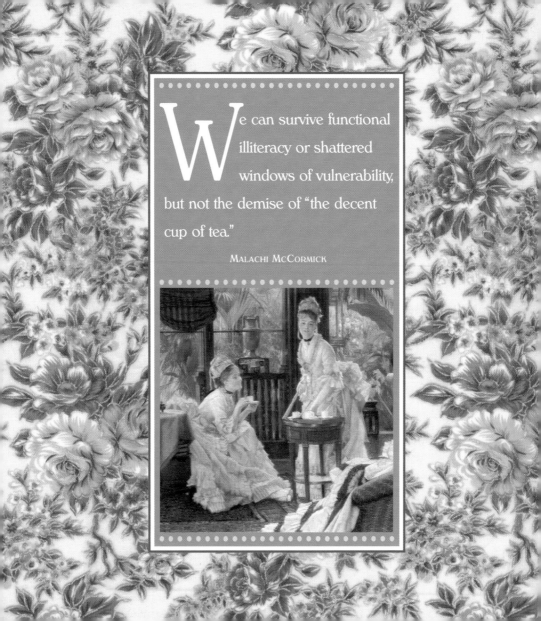